Pioneer Girl

The Story of Laura Ingalls Wilder

Pat Thomson

Contents

OXFORD
UNIVERSITY PRESS

UNIVERSITY PRESS

Great Clarendon Street, Oxford OX2 6DP

Oxford University Press is a department of the University of Oxford.
It furthers the University's objective of excellence in research, scholarship,
and education by publishing worldwide in

Oxford New York

Auckland Cape Town Dar es Salaam Hong Kong Karachi
Kuala Lumpur Madrid Melbourne Mexico City Nairobi
New Delhi Shanghai Taipei Toronto

With offices in

Argentina Austria Brazil Chile Czech Republic France Greece
Guatemala Hungary Italy Japan Poland Portugal Singapore
South Korea Switzerland Thailand Turkey Ukraine Vietnam
Oxford is a registered trade mark of Oxford University Press
in the UK and in certain other countries

British Library Cataloguing in Publication Data

Data available

ISBN: 978 0 19 919540 4

10 9 8 7

True Stories Pack 2 (one of each title) ISBN 0 19 919544 7
True Stories Pack 2 Class Pack (six of each title) ISBN 0 19 919545 5

Acknowledgements

The publisher would like to thank the following for permission
to reproduce photographs:

Laura Ingalls Wilder Memorial Society: pp 3, 28;
Laura Ingalls Wilder Memorial Society/Leslie Kelly: pp 5, 14.

Front cover background artwork : Stone
Inset photo: Laura Ingalls Wilder Memorial Society
Back cover: Laura Ingalls Wilder Memorial Society

Illustrations are by Robin Lawrie

Printed in China by Imago

This is the story of how Laura Ingalls Wilder grew up in America about 120 years ago.

Her **pioneer** father loved to explore new places. This meant they had to make new homes in each different State he took them to.

America was a wild place in those days and that is why Laura had so many adventures.

Laura (third from left) with her parents and her three sisters

Did I ever tell you about the night the wolves howled?

We sat together in our little house made of logs. Outside, the wolves sat in a circle around the house. Our only door was a **quilt**! Yes, a quilt from the bed. It was the only thing between us and the wolves.

But I had better begin at the beginning.

Chapter 1

Our Little House in the Big Woods

I was born in Wisconsin, America, on 7th February 1867.

We lived in a little log house in the middle of the big woods.

There was Pa, Ma, my older sister Mary, and me, Laura Elizabeth Ingalls. My younger sisters, Carrie and Grace, were born later.

This is a **replica** of the "Little House in the Big Woods".

One of the most important members of the family was Jack, our dog. I loved him. He went hunting with Pa and brought home our dinner. He was our guard dog as well.

The big woods were dangerous. There were bears and panthers out there. It was a wild, wild place.

Ma once slapped a bear! It was dark and snowing hard. Ma thought the bear was Sukey, our cow. "Get over," she shouted to the bear. Then we had to run! We were lucky to get back into the house safely and slam the door. Bears are dangerous but this bear was as surprised as we were.

Mary and I helped Ma around the house.
There were no shops. We had to make everything.
Can you guess how we got our sugar? We
drained the **sap** from the maple trees and boiled it.
Then we poured it into pans to harden into
sugar loaves.

However hard it was, we always celebrated Christmas.

In the big woods, we would pour hot maple syrup on the snow to make **candy** shapes.

Chapter 2

Moving West

Pa was a real pioneer. He wanted to travel to the
new lands in the West.

So, one day, in 1869, we left our safe little house in
the woods and set off. Our wagon was waterproof
like a boat, and it had a canvas roof like a tent.
Pa laid his fiddle carefully in the back, but he kept
his gun handy.

Jack had to swim behind the wagon as we
crossed the rivers. There were no bridges then.
We had to cross a river which was flooding.
The wagon started to float.

Pa jumped in and swam, holding the frightened
horses. We just made it to the other side, but Jack
had gone. I thought of poor Jack trying to swim.
I cried.

By the time we camped for the night, the wolves were howling. At bedtime I saw something. There were green eyes shining in the firelight. They came nearer.

Pa raised his gun. The next moment, I screamed!
It was Jack, our Jack, licking my face. He hadn't drowned and he had found us.

Our wagon rolled on across miles of grassland.
We had reached Kansas. This was **Indian** country
– the **prairies**. There were deer in the woods,
rabbits and **prairie chickens** in the grass, and
fish in the rivers.

"There's lots of food here," said Pa. "This is
where we'll build our house."

Chapter 3

Our Little House on the Prairie

This is a replica of the "Little House on the Prairie".

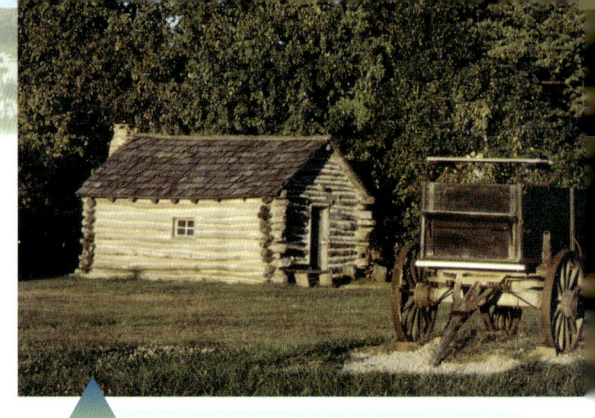

Do you remember I told you about the house where we had a quilt for a door? Well, this was that house.

Soon after those wolves came, Pa made us a wooden door, as well as beds, stools and a table. Inside, I felt safe.

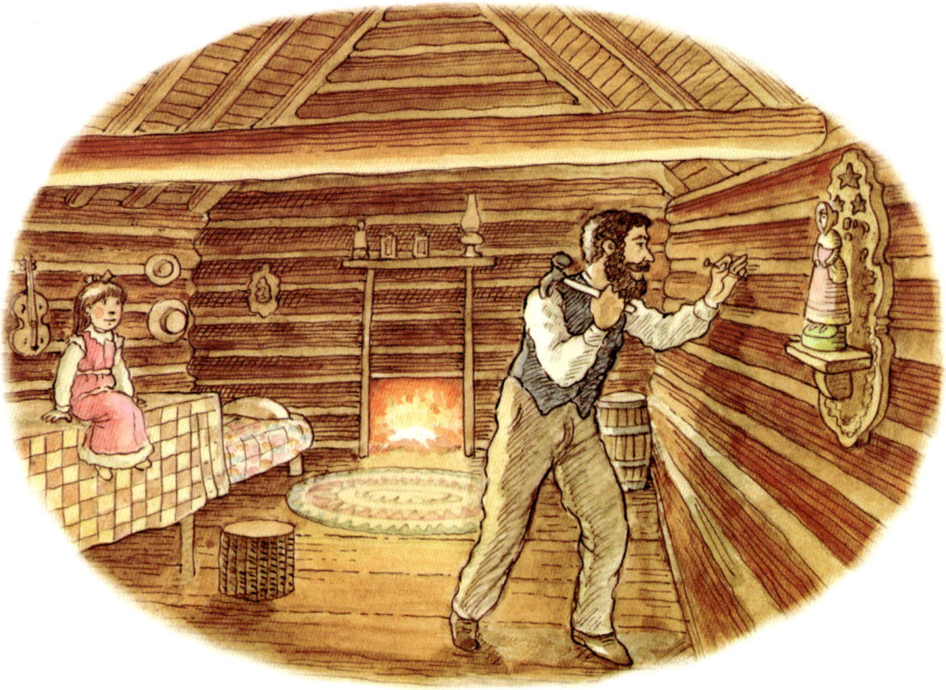

Then, other visitors came. The Indians didn't like us newcomers building houses on their land.

One day when Pa had gone hunting, two fierce-looking men walked into our house. They had feathers in their hair and stood very still.

Ma baked them **cornbread**. We were all silent. Then they left.

Ma was frightened, but Pa said later that the Indians were not our enemies.

A lot happened in the short time we were there. Carrie was born and Ma was ill. Fever and fire swept through the prairies.

Pa wanted to move back to Wisconsin, the place where I was born. Ma agreed. She had started to talk about school. She had once been a teacher and she worried about our schooling.

In 1874 we set off for Walnut Grove, Minnesota.
Pa stopped the wagon. "Here we are," he said.
"But there's nothing here!" said Ma.
"Wait and see!" said Pa.
There was only a grassy river bank, willow trees
and a path leading through the waving grasses.

Chapter 4

Our House on Plum Creek

We followed the path down to the **creek**. There was a door in the bank! We were to live in a home dug out of the bank.

Inside it was dark, but the earth walls and floor were swept smooth. The ceiling was made from willow branches stuffed with hay. The tiny window was greased paper. Our chimney stuck straight out of the grassy bank.

Pa began to grow crops.

We had to start school. After all I was seven now.
It was at school that I met my greatest enemy.

I shall call her Nellie Oleson. She was proud and rich and she was cruel to me. Once she pulled my hair.

But then, one day, I got my own back. She was playing in the creek. I pretended that a big old crab was grabbing Nellie's toes. In she fell! Her fancy clothes were covered in mud.

That was fun, but I have to tell you that, in many ways, it was a sad time.

In summer, grasshoppers came and ate everything Pa had planted.

In winter, terrible **blizzards** froze us.
Ma gave birth to a baby boy – but then he died.
Worst of all, Mary was so ill she became blind.

Chapter 5

Town on the Prairie

After that Pa got a job, in 1879, in Dakota. It was at a rowdy railroad camp. The men who built the new railways were rough and wild.

Ma did not like it. She had baby Grace now and we were older. She still worried about our schooling. It was time to live nearer a town.

So we moved to the town of De Smet. There were real streets and shops. There was even a church.

Pa **claimed** farm land just outside the town. It was free for pioneers like us.

Whenever we met other pioneers, I was shy. After all, I had always lived in wild places and I wasn't used to meeting new people.

That year, the winter was bad. One morning we found the cows with their heads frozen to the ground! They had to be cut free.

It was getting colder and colder and the snowstorms began. They lasted all day and night.

We moved into a house in town, then into one room of the house, trying to keep warm. We huddled round the stove. The food began to run out. There was no more oil for the lamps. Pa was worried. "Even the train can't get through," he said. "We're cut off."

The cold went on and deepened. Christmas dinner that year was a can of soup. We grew thin and weak. Pa stopped playing his fiddle, but he never gave up hope.

One night the roaring wind stopped. Instead, I heard a dripping noise. The ice was melting at last!

That year we had our real Christmas dinner in May, when the first train came with supplies of food.

We went back to our farm in the country and there we stayed for many years.

I did well at school. I even got a job. We were saving up to send Mary to a College for the Blind.

Chapter 6

Writing my Adventures

When I was 15, I became a teacher. Later I married Almanzo Wilder who had brought us food during the blizzard. We had a daughter called Rose. Rose loved to hear my stories, so I began to write about my adventures. One day they would become books for children to read.

Rose in 1920. It was her idea that Laura should write the books.

I wanted to tell children about the things I remembered best.

I remember Jack, of course, those long wagon journeys, and the wild animals and lonely places. Home was where Pa's fiddle was hung on the wall. It was wherever Pa put up a shelf for Ma's china shepherdess. It never got broken.

We were poor, but we made the best of what we had.

When I look back, I remember one thing most of all – we used to sit round the fire, singing, Pa playing his fiddle. It didn't matter where we were. If we were together, we were happy.

Glossary

blizzard   a very bad snowstorm

candy   sweets

claim   a piece of land to live on. The Government gave it to newcomers to encourage them to settle.

cornbread   flat bread made from corn

creek   a stream

Indian   the name which used to be given to the people who lived in North America before white people arrived (now called "Native Americans")

pioneer   the first to do something. In America, a pioneer was someone who settled on new land.

prairies   grasslands

prairie chicken   a wild prairie bird which was good to eat

quilt   a bed cover

replica   a copy of something

sap   the juice of a plant. The sap of a maple tree can be made into maple syrup or hardened into sugar.

Index